XF
JOSEPHS, BEN
Where dinosaurs walked.

Where Dinosaurs Walked

by Ben Josephs

Reading Consultant: Wiley Blevins, M.A.
Phonics/Early Reading Specialist

 COMPASS POINT BOOKS

Minneapolis, Minnesota

Compass Point Books
3109 West 50th Street, #115
Minneapolis, MN 55410

Visit Compass Point Books on the Internet at *www.compasspointbooks.com*
or e-mail your request to *custserv@compasspointbooks.com*

Photographs ©: Cover and p. 1: Photo of Dilophosaurus diorama at the Dinosaur State Park,
Rocky Hill, CT by McConnell & McNamara/Jack McConnell, p. 6: Image Ideas, Inc./Bruce
Ando, p. 7: Bruce Coleman, Inc./Michael Fogden, p. 8 (left): Corbis/Manuel Bellver,
p. 8 (right): Bruce Coleman, Inc./Alex Kerstitch, p. 9: Corbis/Bettmann, p. 10: The Natural
History Museum/Orbis, p. 11: Index Stock Imagery/RO-MA Stock, p. 12: Index Stock
Imagery/Jeff Greenberg

Editorial Development: Alice Dickstein, Alice Boynton
Photo Researcher: Wanda Winch
Design/Page Production: Silver Editions, Inc.

Library of Congress Cataloging-in-Publication Data
Josephs, Ben.
   Where dinosaurs walked / by Ben Josephs.
      p. cm. — (Compass Point phonics readers)
Includes index.
Summary: Discusses the fossils left by dinosaurs in an easy-to-read text
that incorporates phonics instruction and rebuses.
   ISBN 0-7565-0531-3 (hardcover : alk. paper)
   1. Dinosaurs—Juvenile literature. 2. Reading—Phonetic
method—Juvenile literature. [1. Dinosaurs. 2. Rebuses. 3.
Reading—Phonetic method.] I. Title. II. Series.
   QE861.5.J67 2004
   567.9—dc21   2003006378

Table of Contents

Dear Parent or Caregiver,

Welcome to Compass Point Phonics Readers, books of information for young children. Each book concentrates on specific phonic sounds and words commonly found in beginning reading materials. Featuring eye-catching photographs, every book explores a single science or social studies concept that is sure to grab a child's interest.

So snuggle up with your child, and let's begin. Start by reading aloud the Mother Goose nursery rhyme on the next page. As you read, stress the words in dark type. These are the words that contain the phonic sounds featured in this book. After several readings, pause before the rhyming words, and let your child chime in.

Now let's read *Where Dinosaurs Walked*. If your child is a beginning reader, have him or her first read it silently. Then ask your child to read it aloud. For children who are not yet reading, read the book aloud as you run your finger under the words. Ask your child to imitate, or "echo," what he or she has just heard.

Discussing the book's content with your child:
Explain to your child that scientists matched the footprints of Dilophosaurus (die · LOH · fuh · SAW · rus) and Coelophysis (SEE · loh · FIE · sis) with skeletons found in other places to identify the dinosaurs with reasonable certainty.

At the back of the book is a fun Nice Going! game. Your child will take pride in demonstrating his or her mastery of the phonic sounds and the high-frequency words.

Enjoy Compass Point Phonics Readers and watch your child read and learn!

One Day

One day a boy went **walking**
And **walked** into a store.
He bought a pound of **sausage** meat
And laid it on the floor.
The boy began to whistle—
He whistled up a tune,
And **all** the little **sausages**
Danced around the room.

One day, a worker was digging a deep hole. He was amazed by what he saw. There were huge footprints in the rock. They were made by **dinosaurs**.

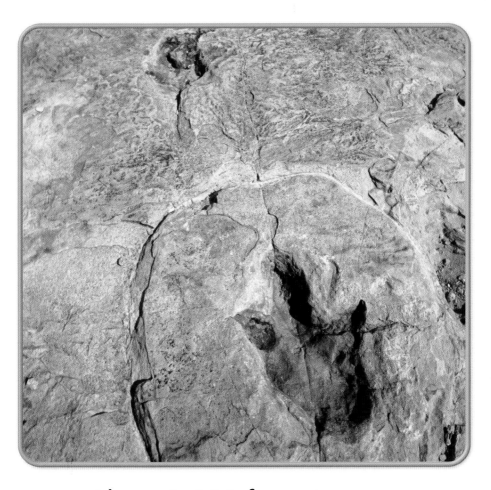

About 2,000 footprints were found! Today, people from all over visit that place. They want to see where dinosaurs walked millions of years ago.

plant fossil

animal fossil

The dinosaur footprints are called **fossils**. Fossils are parts or prints of animals and plants that lived long ago. Fossils teach us about life in the past.

Scientists came and looked at the footprints. They saw the size of each one. They counted the toes. They could tell which kinds of dinosaurs had made the footprints.

Some footprints were made
by Dilophosaurus. Each back foot
had 3 toes with sharp claws.
Dilophosaurus was a tall
dinosaur. Maybe it looked like this.

Some footprints were made by
Coelophysis. Each back foot had
3 long toes and 1 short toe.
    Coelophysis was a smaller
dinosaur. Maybe it looked like this.

Dinosaur footprints can be found in many places. Go and see them, if you can. Draw them, too. Match your hands or feet with those footprints made long ago.

Word List

Variant Vowel /ô/
a, au, aw

a (I, II)
walked
all
called
smaller
tall

au
dinosaur(s)

aw
claws
draw
saw

High-Frequency
could

Science
Coelophysis
Dilophosaurus
dinosaur(s)
millions
scientists

Nice Going!

Player 1

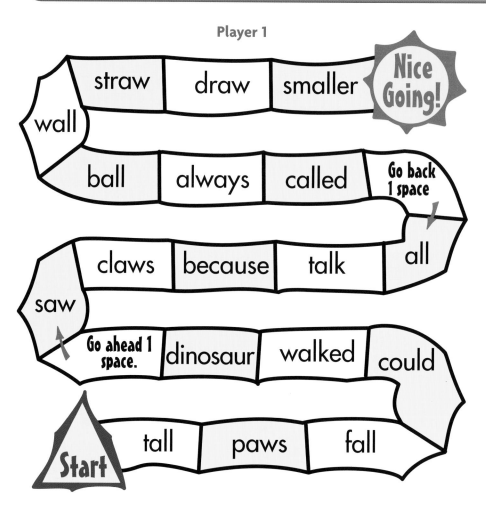

straw · draw · smaller · Nice Going!

wall

ball · always · called · Go back 1 space

claws · because · talk · all

saw · Go ahead 1 space. · dinosaur · walked · could

Start · tall · paws · fall

14

How to Play

- Each player puts a moving piece on his or her Start. Players take turns shaking the penny and dropping it on the table. Heads means move 1 space. Tails means move 2 spaces.
- The player moves and reads the word in the space. If the child cannot read the word, tell him or her what it is. On the next turn, the child must read the word before moving.
- If a player lands on a space having special directions, he or she should move accordingly.
- The first player to reach the *Nice Going!* sign wins the game.

Player 2

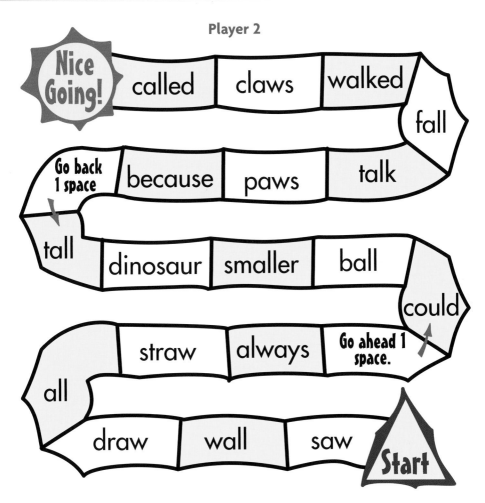

Read More

Dodson, Peter. *An Alphabet of Dinosaurs*. New York: Scholastic, 1995.

Matthews, Rupert. *Tyrannosaurus Rex*. Gone Forever Series. Chicago, Ill.: Heinemann Library, 2003.

Scott, Janine. *Discovering Dinosaurs*. Spyglass Books Series. Minneapolis, Minn.: Compass Point Books, 2002.

Stewart, Melissa. *Fossils*. Simply Science Series. Minneapolis, Minn.: Compass Point Books, 2003.

Index